EYEWITNESS
VICTORIANS

Kitchen utensils

Ironworker

Punch and Judy puppets

Queen Victoria's parasol

Mangle

BOVRIL

Wall advertisement

Victoria and Albert's wedding

Salvation Army bonnet

EYEWITNESS
VICTORIANS

Memorial newspaper

Written by
ANN KRAMER

Geometric shapes

Mrs Beeton's *Book of Household Management*

Christmas card

Portmanteau and hatbox

Playing cards

Ruby lustre tile

Egg and dart
cornice

Servant's
bell

DK | Penguin Random House

Project editor Claire Bampton
Art editor Lesley Betts
Picture research Melissa Albany,
Marianna Sonnenburg, Helen Stallion
Photographers John Chase, Andy Crawford
Illustrators Adam Abel, Lee Montgomery
Editorial consultant Aan Wilkinson

RELAUNCH EDITION (DK UK)
Editor Ashwin Khurana
Managing editor Gareth Jones
Managing art editor Philip Letsu
Publisher Andrew Macintyre
Producer, pre-production Adam Stoneham
Senior producer Janis Griffith
Jacket editor Maud Whatley
Jacket designer Laura Brim
Jacket development manager Sophia MTT
Publishing director Jonathan Metcalf
Associate publishing director Liz Wheeler
Art director Phil Ormerod

RELAUNCH EDITION (DK INDIA)
Editor Ishani Nandi
Project art editor Deep Shikha Walia
Art editor Amit Varma
DTP designer Pawan Kumar
Senior DTP designer Harish Aggarwal
Managing editor Alka Thakur Hazarika
Managing art editor Romi Chakraborty
CTS manager Balwant Singh
Jacket designers Suhita Dharamjit, Sukriti Sobti
Managing jacket editor Saloni Singh

This Eyewitness ® Guide has been conceived by
Dorling Kindersley Limited and Editions Gallimard

Hardback edition first published in Great Britain in 1998
This edition published in Great Britain in 2015 by
Dorling Kindersley Limited, 80 Strand, London WC2R 0RL

Copyright © 1998, © 2003, © 2008, © 2015
Dorling Kindersley Limited
A Penguin Random House Company

2 4 6 8 10 9 7 5 3 1 001 – 280088 — 03/15

ISBN 978-0-2411-8759-3

Colour reproduction by Alta Image Ltd, London, UK
Printed and bound by South China Printing Co Ltd, China

A WORLD OF IDEAS:
SEE ALL THERE IS TO KNOW

Family
photographs

City of
London fire
bucket

Child's
toy

Lemonade and
beer bottles

Home remedies

Contents

Sheet music

Commemorative fan

Queen Victoria

Queen Victoria came to the throne in 1837. She ruled for more than 63 years and is the longest-reigning British monarch. Her reign saw enormous change as Britain built up the world's biggest empire, the largest navy, and the most modern industries. When Victoria died in 1901, she was a symbol of British greatness and much loved. Her reign is known as the Victorian Age and British people of the time as Victorians.

A princess's life

Victoria grew up in Kensington Palace, London. Her mother was overly protective, her upbringing was strict, and she had few companions.

Becoming Queen

Victoria was only 18 years old when she became Queen, but took to her duties with enthusiasm and determination. Within hours, she attended her first official meeting with leading politicians.

Duties as Queen

As a constitutional monarch, Victoria could not decide affairs of state. Real political power lay with Parliament. But she worked closely with her ministers, and was interested in the progress of the Empire.

Marriage to Albert

In 1840, Victoria married her German cousin, Albert. She was devoted to her "dear Angel", who was her closest companion and adviser.

Queen Victoria's sketchbook

Princess Victoria's music book

Victoria sketched people and places from memory

Sketch of the Scottish Highlands

Hobbies and interests

Throughout her early and married life, Victoria loved music, dancing, sketching, and, later on, riding. She also kept a diary from the age of 13 until her death.

The sceptre is a symbol of authority

Victoria was only 1.5 m (5 ft) tall, but had an imposing personality

Queen Victoria 1819–1901

Victoria's life spanned most of the 19th century, and her family, or dynasty, still rules Britain today. Queen Elizabeth II is her great great granddaughter.

1819
Birth
24 May: Victoria is born. Her father, the Duke of Kent, and his father, King George III, die the following year.

1837
Queen
20 June: Victoria becomes Queen on the death of her uncle, William IV. She is his only heir, and is crowned a year later.

1840
Marriage
10 February: Victoria marries her German cousin Albert, Duke of Saxe-Coburg-Gotha.

Crown

Crown jewels

Victoria in her coronation robes, aged 19

Queen Victoria by
Sir George Hayter

Family life

Victoria and Albert had nine children – five daughters and four sons. Royal duties allowing, they spent as much time as possible with their children, and their close-knit home life impressed the British public. Many of their 37 grandchildren married into royal houses across Europe.

Of Victoria's nine children, three died before their mother: Alice, Leopold, and Alfred

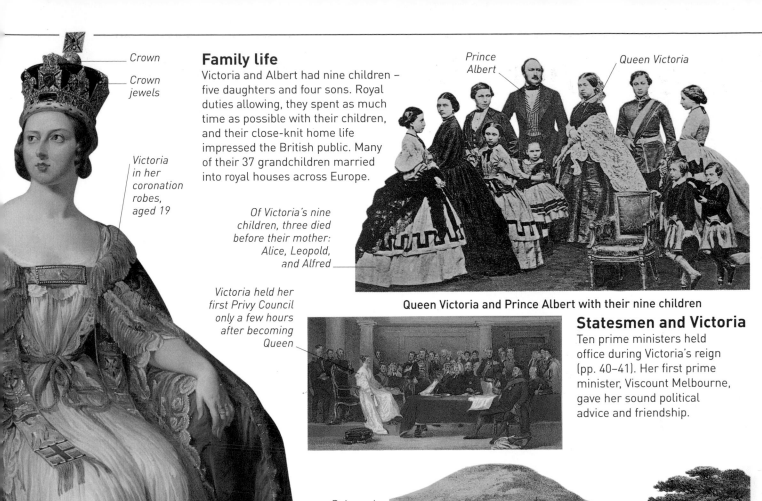

Prince Albert

Queen Victoria

Queen Victoria and Prince Albert with their nine children

Victoria held her first Privy Council only a few hours after becoming Queen

Statesmen and Victoria

Ten prime ministers held office during Victoria's reign (pp. 40–41). Her first prime minister, Viscount Melbourne, gave her sound political advice and friendship.

Balmoral Castle was Queen Victoria's favourite home

Castle retreat

When Victoria became Queen, she moved into Buckingham Palace. During the 1840s, she and Albert bought and restored two family homes: Osborne House on the Isle of Wight, and Balmoral Castle in the Scottish Highlands. After Albert's death, Victoria spent much time at Balmoral, grieving in the company of her closest servant, the Scotsman John Brown.

1861
Widowhood
Albert dies from typhoid. Victoria is heartbroken, and withdraws from public life for the next 13 years.

1876
Empress of India
From the early 1870s, Victoria resumes public duties. In 1876, Parliament gives her the title "Empress of India".

1897
Diamond Jubilee
Now in a wheelchair and suffering from rheumatism, Victoria celebrates 60 years on the throne. She is hugely popular.

1901
Death
22 January: Victoria dies, and is buried next to Albert at Windsor Castle. The Empire mourns her death.

Industrial might

The Industrial Revolution had begun in Britain in the late 18th century. New, steam-driven machinery could do the work of many people, and the manufacture of goods in new factories enabled mass production. In the Victorian period, the pace of change intensified, transforming British society, and made Britain the world's first, and most powerful, industrial nation.

The Shingling Hammer
by William McConnell

Raw materials

Coal and iron made the Industrial Revolution possible. Coal furnaces boiled water to produce steam, which drove new machines. Coal stimulated iron and steel production and powered locomotives and ships.

Iron working

In 1828, the development of a coal-powered, hot-blast furnace made iron working cheaper. This and a new steam-driven hammer, which shaped iron with power and precision, helped produce new goods, from railway tracks to machinery.

Iron ore

Britain was
rich in coal

Wrought iron
rod, shaped by
hammering

Ladle to skim
impurities from
molten iron

Iron bars

Iron was used
to make new
machinery

Steel age

Steel is stronger and less brittle than cast iron. In 1856, Henry Bessemer invented a converter that produced steel easily. In 1866, the Siemens open-hearth steel furnace allowed steel to be produced in bulk. From the 1860s, ships, boilers, and huge structures, such as bridges, were made from steel.

Cotton mills

Mechanization reached the textile industry first. In the 18th century, machines such as the spinning jenny had begun to replace manual spinning wheels and looms. Water powered the new machines until steam replaced it in the 1790s. Cotton became Britain's leading industry and was traded worldwide.

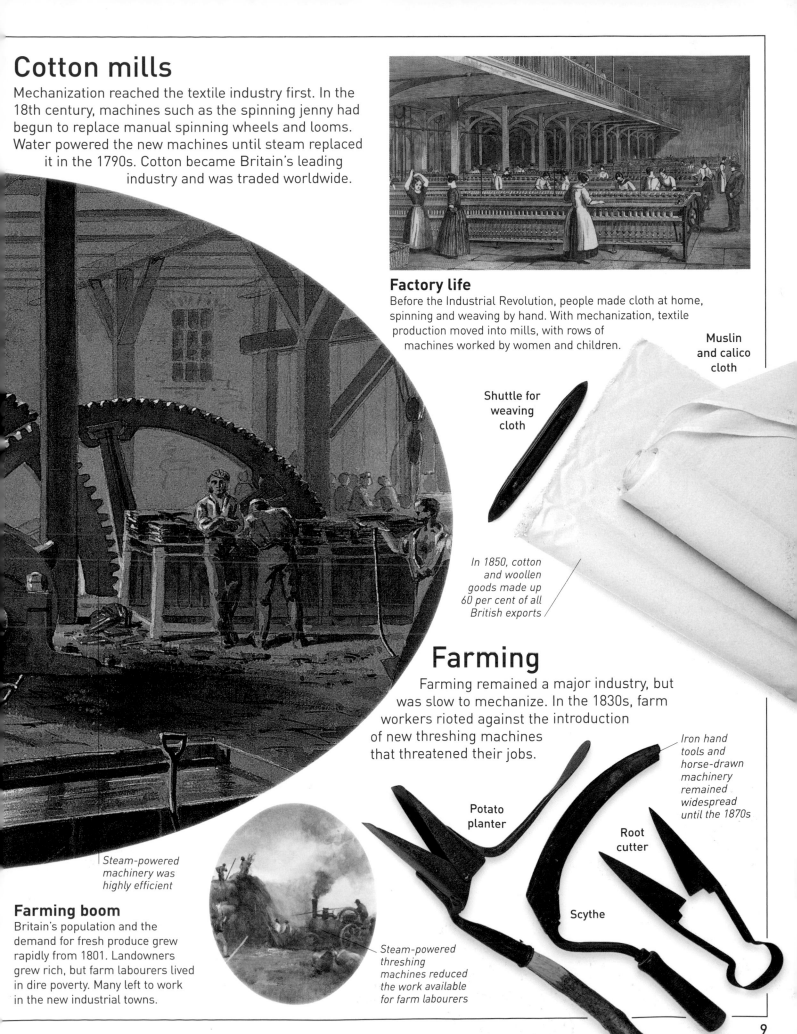

Factory life
Before the Industrial Revolution, people made cloth at home, spinning and weaving by hand. With mechanization, textile production moved into mills, with rows of machines worked by women and children.

Muslin and calico cloth

Shuttle for weaving cloth

In 1850, cotton and woollen goods made up 60 per cent of all British exports

Farming

Farming remained a major industry, but was slow to mechanize. In the 1830s, farm workers rioted against the introduction of new threshing machines that threatened their jobs.

Iron hand tools and horse-drawn machinery remained widespread until the 1870s

Potato planter

Root cutter

Scythe

Steam-powered machinery was highly efficient

Farming boom
Britain's population and the demand for fresh produce grew rapidly from 1801. Landowners grew rich, but farm labourers lived in dire poverty. Many left to work in the new industrial towns.

Steam-powered threshing machines reduced the work available for farm labourers

The railways

Transport of all kinds, on land and sea, developed rapidly in the Victorian period, but the arrival of the railways had the biggest impact on British society. By moving raw materials and finished goods quickly around the country, railways boosted industries, trade, employment, the growth of towns, and a new world of travel. Goods, people, mail, and ideas travelled faster than ever before.

A great engineer

One of the greatest Victorian engineers, Isambard Kingdom Brunel created the Great Western Railway, planned the Clifton Suspension Bridge, and designed the *Great Western*, the first trans-Atlantic steamship, as well as the *Great Britain*, the first screw-propelled, ocean steamship.

Isambard Kingdom Brunel

Steam power

In 1803, the first steam railway locomotive was invented. Coal burned in a boiler and heated water to produce the steam that powered the engine.

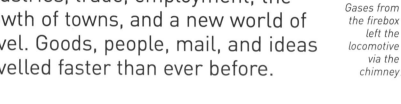

Gases from the firebox left the locomotive via the chimney

Steam whistle

Columbine steam locomotive

Steam drove the pistons back and forth

Piston, linked to rod

Rod drove wheels around

Navvies worked with picks, shovels, and barrows

Building the railways

Railway planners such as George Stephenson and Isambard Kingdom Brunel hired huge gangs of skilled workmen, known as navvies, to build tracks, bridges, tunnels, and embankments.

Workman's shovel

Workman's pick

The navvies

Some 250,000 navvies built the Victorian railways. Named after the "navigators" who had built the canals in the 18th century, they lived in shantytowns beside the tracks.

19th-century transport

Before the 1830s, people travelled long distances in horse-drawn transport. In the Victorian period, forms of public transport changed dramatically.

1850s
Double-decker bus

In 1829, the first horse-drawn omnibus appeared in London. By 1850, buses were open-topped double-deckers. By 1902, motor buses had replaced them.

1863
Underground

The world's first underground railway opened in London in 1863. Steam engines pulled carriages along the roofed trenches.

Railway "mania"

Most of Britain's railways were built during the 1840s and 1850s. Private individuals built separate lines, forming companies to raise money. Shareholders then shared in the profits. During the railway "mania" of the 1840s, people made profit from investing in the railways. By the 1850s, the boom, and profits, were over.

Great Western Railway station master's hat

Lancashire and Yorkshire Railway whistle

London, Chatham, and Dover Railway insignia

By opening the regulator valve the train was propelled forwards or backwards

Railway stations

Stations appeared as railway lines arrived in different cities. This painting, *The Railway Station* (1853) by English artist William Frith, captures the excitement and bustle of the Victorian station at Paddington, in London.

Holidays by train

In 1842, Queen Victoria made her first train journey. Soon, increasing numbers of people used trains to travel to work and go on holiday, and seaside resorts were developed.

Coal burned in the firebox

The train driver stood here

Coal regulator to stem the flow of coal

Coal was stored in this truck

1868

Coupling rod

First-class compartment

Train ticket

Travelling conditions

Early trains were uncomfortable. Third-class carriages were little more than boxes on wheels. In the 1870s, upholstered seats were fitted. Steam heating came in 1884, and restaurant cars in 1892.

Cost and speed

Train travel was faster and cheaper than long-distance horse travel. From 1844, third-class travel cost a penny a mile (1.6 km). By 1895, speeds averaged 112 kph (69.5 mph).

Ticket clippers

1870
Penny-farthing
The first pedal bicycles appeared in 1839. Later, "penny-farthings" were popular. By 1885, bicycles had equal-sized wheels and a safety chain.

1885
Electric tramcar
Horse-drawn tramcars on rails came into use in the 1860s. Later, steam replaced horses. The first electric tram hit Blackpool in 1885.

1886
Motor taxicab
The first successful car, made in Germany in 1886, looked like a horseless carriage. Gradually motor cars spread to Britain, too.

A great exhibition

In a period of extraordinary economic growth between 1815 and the 1870s, Britain exported goods worldwide and became known as "the workshop of the world". To celebrate and promote this success, the Great Exhibition was held in 1851. It was the first international exhibition and a monument to Victorian achievement.

The Crystal Palace

The centrepiece of the Great Exhibition was the exhibition hall itself. Designed by architect Joseph Paxton, it was made from iron and glass, and nicknamed "Crystal Palace".

Joseph Paxton

Great Exhibition season ticket

Railway excursions
Special excursion trains ran from industrial towns to London, so that workers could visit the exhibition.

Royal spectacle

On 1 May 1851, Queen Victoria and Prince Albert opened the Great Exhibition in Hyde Park, London. The six-month exhibition was a hit, hailed as "the grandest spectacle the world has ever witnessed".

The hall consisted of prefabricated "units", made in factories and brought by train

Each unit was bolted, screwed, or slotted into place

The building was 550 m (1,804 ft) long and 140 m (459 ft) wide at its broadest point

The Crystal Palace was the first large public building to have public lavatories

Inside the exhibition
The main exhibition hall in the Crystal Palace was vast. It covered 9,300 sq m (100,104 sq ft) and its glass-topped ceiling was 19 m (62 ft) high. More than 100,000 exhibits were on show.

Crowds of visitors
Attracting more than six million visitors, the Great Exhibition made a profit. The money was used to build new museums, colleges, and the Royal Albert Hall.

Victorian inventions

The Great Exhibition marked a high point of British optimism. The Victorians were inventive and practical and loved using the inventions of their age.

1844
Morse telegraph
Five years after a British patent for a telegraph, US inventor Samuel Morse sent the first successful telegraph message, using dots and dashes.

1855
Printing telegraph
In 1839, railways used telegraphs for the first time. By 1855, news items and other urgent messages were being wired around the world.

1873
Typewriter
The first commercial typewriter was produced in 1873 and soon began to replace pen and ink in the office. By 1900, most typists were women.

Exhibits galore

Visitors to the Crystal Palace marvelled at the wealth of exhibits. The stands were arranged in walk-in galleries on three levels, and contained the latest farming and industrial technology.

Flags of all nations flew from the roof

The high central vault enclosed two tall elm trees

A cast-iron frame supported 300,000 glass panes

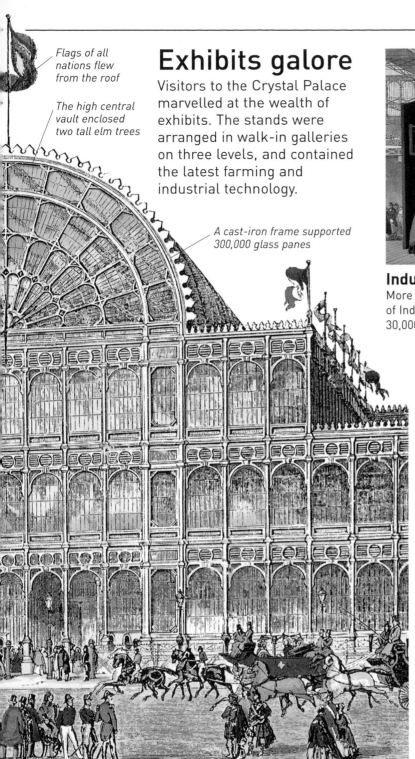

Industry of all nations

More than half the exhibits were British, alongside "the Works of Industry of all Nations", such as China (above). More than 30,000 international exhibitors – and visitors – took part.

Industry and art

The thousands of exhibits were divided into four main categories: raw materials, machinery, manufactured goods, and fine arts. Machinery was the main focus of interest, but the Great Exhibition included an enormous range of arts and crafts, some of it highly decorative.

Frontispiece of "The Park and the Crystal Palace"

Ornate French clock

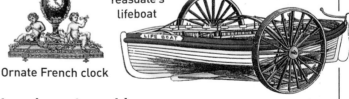

Teasdale's lifeboat

Food and drink

Visitors could buy a huge range of food and drink, from sandwiches and tea to ices made by a steam-powered freezer.

Jewels and machinery

Exhibits ranged from the magnificent Koh-i-noor diamond to James Nasmyth's great steam hammer and a medal-making machine that Queen Victoria admired.

1879
Telephone
Alexander Bell patented the telephone in 1876. Three years later, Thomas Edison produced this wall-mounted phone. By 1900, there were 210,000 telephones in Britain.

1881
Electric lighting
In 1879, Thomas Edison and Britain's Joseph Swan independently invented the light bulb. Electric street lighting appeared in 1881.

1888
Record player
US inventor Emile Berliner developed the first disc record player, which soon began to appear in wealthy Victorian homes.

Working lives

Life was grim for working people during the first half of Victoria's reign. Huge numbers of people went to work in factories, foundries, and mills, where wages were low and conditions appalling. Others were employed in mines and workshops. From the 1850s, trade and industry expanded rapidly and working conditions improved.

Men at work

From the 1850s, new "skilled" occupations appeared, such as boiler-making, shipbuilding, and engineering. Men in these industries, together with miners and railway workers, were known as the "aristocracy of labour". Labourers and dockers were "unskilled".

Health and safety

With no laws safeguarding workers' health and safety, factories and foundries were dangerous places. Workers suffered accidents, burns, and toxic fumes. With no pensions or benefits, unemployment meant poverty. People worked for as long as they could.

Ironworkers were skilled workers

The lid was used as a teacup

Workers heated a billycan over a fire to make tea

Sandwich tin filled with bread and dripping (fat)

Workers took their own lunch to work

Some employers supplied candles

The working day

Most people today work an eight-hour day. In Victorian factories, workers, often after a long walk to work, toiled for up to 18 hours. From the 1830s, reformers campaigned for a maximum of ten hours a day.

Rules and regulations were strict and usually favoured the employer

RULES & REGULATIONS
FOR ALL
WORKMEN, APPRENTICES, AND BOYS
EMPLOYED ON
THESE PREMISES

All Persons are engaged on condition that they observe the following Rules and Regulations

John Edmunds Printer, Blists Hill

Child labour

In Victorian Britain, children made up more than 25 per cent of the labour force. Thousands worked in workshops, factories, and mines, where they pulled coal wagons and cleaned under the constantly moving machines. Accidents and deaths were common.

Fines and wages

Employers often fined workers, even for whistling. Some paid only with goods, or tokens that could be used only at the company store.

Ironworkers repaired tools and carts, and made items from wrought iron

Women at work

Women worked as servants, needleworkers, and in textile mills. They were paid less than men. Some men opposed women's work, scared that their pay would drop, too.

Pennies

A PLAIN COOKERY BOOK FOR THE WORKING CLASSES BY CHARLES ELMÉ FRANCATELLI LATE MAITRE D'HÔTEL AND CHIEF COOK TO HER GRACIOUS MAJESTY QUEEN VICTORIA PRYOR PUBLICATIONS WHITSTABLE AND WALSALL

Cookery book

Traditionally, whole families were miners

Seamstresses worked for up to 15 hours a day, sewing by hand

Double burden
Working women also had to go home to clean and care for their families. Victorians wanted wives to stay home, but many could not afford to.

Pitbrow lassies
Victorians were shocked by women miners working in such dangerous conditions and in close contact with men. In 1842, women and children were banned from underground work. Some women continued working overground until the 1880s.

Weary and worn
Some of the most poorly paid Victorian workers were seamstresses, who worked incredibly long hours, stitching clothes for the rich with just a needle and thread.

Victorian **cotton reels**

Seamstresses' hands were pricked, sore, and bleeding

Before the invention of the sewing machine in 1851, every item of clothing was sewn by hand

Factory reform
In the early 1800s, many employers feared that better conditions would damage production. Official enquiries gradually led to reform.

1833
Factory Act bans children under nine from working in factories and mills. No night work for people under 18.

1842
Women, girls, and boys under 10 are banned from underground work.

1844
Children aged 9 to 13 are to work no more than 6.5 hours a day; 13- to 18-year-olds and women are to work no more than 12 hours a day.

1847
Women and young people in factories are to work no more than 10 hours a day. In 1864–78, reforms extend from textile mills to other industries.

Living conditions
As industrial towns developed, workers' houses were built quickly and cheaply, often with no running water or bathrooms. Several families lived in one room, and disease was common.

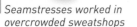

Seamstresses worked in overcrowded sweatshops

Victorian cities

Towns and cities grew rapidly and the population soared. In 1801, 33 per cent of the British population lived in towns. By 1901, the figure was 78 per cent. London and the cities of the industrial north saw the most growth. Pollution, poor housing, and lack of public amenities and services caused dreadful conditions.

A consumer society

Growing prosperity led to an increasing range of shops and consumer items. Manufacturers began to advertise their wares, and department stores appeared, such as Harrods in London.

Tin advertising plates

Provision department at Harrods

Display made up of cans of food

Street life

Many cities were seriously overcrowded, and suffered air pollution from factories, or water pollution from open sewers and lack of sanitation. But city centres also bustled with horse-drawn carriages, street sellers, shops, banks, and theatres.

Orange seller

Street traders

A vast army of people earned their living on the streets, selling fruit, vegetables, snacks, and drinks. Children earned pennies by sweeping streets at every crossing.

Ginger beer seller

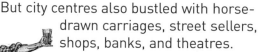

Markets

This painting, *A Busy Market* by Alfred H. Green, shows stalls selling fish and other goods. Trains brought fresh food from the countryside into towns.

Slums and suburbs

Poor families were crammed into cellars or tall tenements. Wealthier families lived in villas and terraces in more select areas. Middle-class families increasingly moved out to the suburbs.

Carts, omnibuses, and cabs were pulled by horses

Trams ran on lines through the streets

Improving cities

Overcrowding, poverty, and lack of sanitation caused frequent outbreaks of fatal diseases such as cholera and typhoid. In 1848, the first Public Health Act was passed. Gradually, sewers were built, clean water was piped to many homes, and street cleaning and lighting were introduced.

Bandstand at Clapham Common, London

Band members wore uniforms

Civic pride

From the 1850s, local authorities and businessmen built imposing municipal buildings, such as town halls and libraries, or funded public parks. Every park had a bandstand where, on Sundays, brass bands played popular tunes as families strolled by.

Bobbies on the beat

In 1829, Sir Robert Peel set up the first metropolitan police force in London. Known as "peelers" or "bobbies", the new policemen wore uniforms and patrolled their areas. By 1856, most towns had a police force.

The Cross, Eastgate St, Chester by Louise Rayner

The production of more varied goods, in the 1860s, gave rise to more shops in the cities

Local authorities introduced street lighting

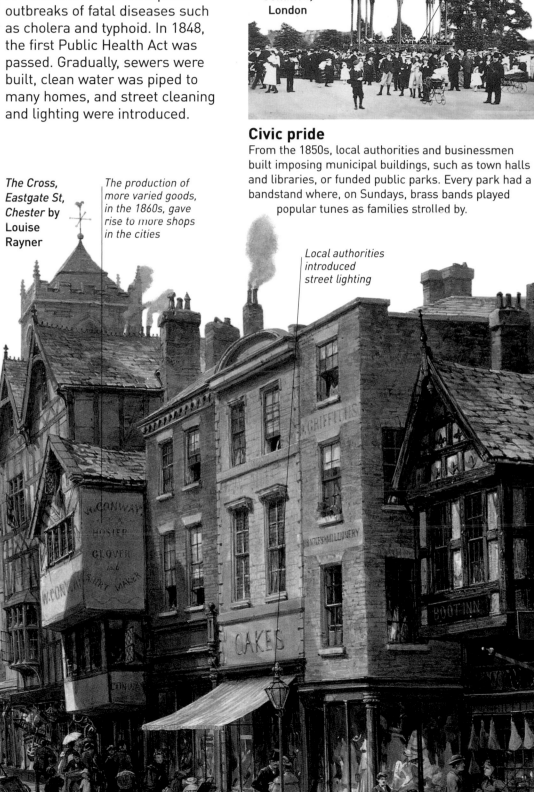

City of London Fire Brigade equipment

City of London crest

Firefighters put out fires with buckets of water

Fire-fighting axe with extra-long handle

From the 1860s pavements were improved

Public services

In 1835, the Municipal Corporation Act set up a new system of local government. Town councils elected by local ratepayers could raise money and provide social services such as police, firefighters, lighting, and housing.

In the home

For the Victorians, the family was central to their lives. The home was seen as a refuge from the world of work, and a woman's role was to provide comfort and support. Taking their lead from the royal family, the middle classes developed an ideal of what family life should be: peaceful, harmonious, and highly respectable.

Home life

Families spent much of their time in the drawing room, where they received guests and gathered to play music, read, enjoy games, and talk.

Indoor entertainment

In an age before television, families played card games, such as Happy Families, word games, and board games such as Ludo. They also read aloud to one another from novels.

Journal containing short story

Christmas candles

It became common for families to send Christmas cards to one another

Christmas cheer

It was at this time that Christmas became an important family occasion. Prince Albert introduced the German custom of having a decorated tree and presents. Christmas cards were first sold in 1846.

Victorian children

Families were often quite large, with as many as six or seven children. Children were treated strictly and were expected to be seen, not heard.

Snakes and ladders board game

Child's box toy

Hand-painted mechanical tin toy

Nurseries

Nannies looked after young children in the nursery, organizing their lessons, games, walks, and meals. Obedience was essential.

The aim is to get the ball into the cup, without touching the ball

Cup and ball game

Jigsaw puzzles were for the whole family

LATEST PICTURE PUZZLE.
THE "TORMENTUM"
A.W. GAMAGE. LTD HOLBORN E.C.

Victorian homes were heated with coal fires

Women were expected to wear formal dress at home as well as outdoors

Christmas cards

Family roles

The father was head of the family. His role was to go to work and provide for the family. A woman's place was in the home. Until 1882, a married woman's property belonged to her husband. Her role was to be a good wife and mother. From the 1840s, some middle-class women campaigned for greater freedom.

Sunday best

Religion played an important part in Victorian family life. On Sundays, the whole family went to church, and in the evening the father read aloud from the Bible.

Outside the home gentlemen wore top hats and carried walking sticks

Sheet music

Walking stick

Victorian women carried parasols when outdoors

Home Sweet Home by Walter Dendy Sadler

Embroidery and cross-stitch were seen as suitable pastimes for women

Children dressed in formal clothes, just like adults

Musical evenings

Every Victorian drawing room had a piano. All young women learned to play, and in the evenings the family gathered round to sing popular ballads such as "Home Sweet Home".

19

Life below stairs

Middle-class homes would not have survived without servants to do the work. Every upper- and middle-class family had servants. While some homes had only a single maidservant, others employed a whole army. Life was hard. Without running hot water, washing machines, or vacuum cleaners, all housework had to be done by hand.

Household advice

Running a household involved careful organization. The housekeeper or mistress instructed the servants. Women referred to Mrs Beeton's *Book of Household Management*.

Best-seller
Isabella Beeton was 21 when she started writing her book. First published in 1861, it was the essential home guide. By 1871, it had sold two million copies.

Mrs Beeton's book gives more than 1,300 recipes

Daily duties
A maid's daily duties included cleaning and lighting the kitchen range, emptying slop buckets, scrubbing steps, polishing boots, and cleaning the entire house.

Egg whisk

Butter stamp

Jelly mould

Mixing bowl and wooden spoon

Cook
The cook worked hard all day, preparing meals by hand for the family and the servants. Victorian middle-class menus included soups, joints of meat, fish, fresh vegetables, and puddings.

Heavy iron kettle

Water was heated on the kitchen range in a kettle or a copper pan

Scullery maid
Young girls started in service as scullery or kitchen maids as soon as they left school. They worked long hours for little or no pay, and sometimes only for board and lodging.

Household inventions

Technology led to the development of domestic appliances. They replaced servants, but not until the 20th century. The flushing lavatory, invented in 1778, was used in wealthy homes.

1854
Paraffin lamp
Oil, or paraffin lamps, invented in about 1854, provided a better light than flickering candles.

1855
Can opener

Canned foods replaced salting or freezing as ways to preserve food. Cans came with can-openers.

1882
Electric iron

In 1882, the cordless electric iron was invented.

Suitable work for women

In 1871, more than a third of British women aged 12–20 years old were "in service". Young women often hated the long hours, constant orders, and lack of freedom.

Black-lead was actually graphite, a type of carbon

Stove brush

Open fires

Every morning, the housemaid swept out the ashes, brushed, black-leaded, and polished the iron ranges and fire grates, then laid and lit the coal.

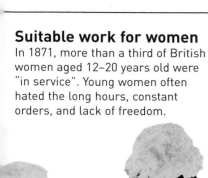

Cook and kitchen maids at work

Maids wore starched caps

White starched apron

Kitchen maids bought food fresh each day because there were no refrigerators

Kitchen staff spent all day below stairs

Low wages

Servants worked 15 to 18 hours a day, with only half a day off a week. Lodging came with the job, but pay was low. According to Mrs Beeton, servants could earn between £9 to £25 a year.

The butler was usually served first

The servants' hall

Wealthy households had many servants: a housekeeper, cooks, a butler, maids, kitchen boys, gardeners, and perhaps coachmen. Servants were ranked by importance, wore different uniforms, and followed a strict code of behaviour.

BORAX
SELF GLAZING
WHITE
POWDER
STARCH

Blue Bag was used to make washing whiter

Flat iron

Bar of soap

PURITAN SOAP

The iron had to be heated on the range

Wooden pegs

Washing and cleaning

Everything – rooms, ornaments, linen, the family's clothes – had to be spotless. Maids dusted and swept daily. Laundresses did the washing. Ironing meant using flat irons that had been heated on the range.

1889
Vacuum cleaner

Early models of the vacuum cleaner, such as this one from 1889, blew dust away rather than sucked it up. In 1901, the first suction vacuum cleaner was made.

1891
Electric oven

In 1879, an electric oven was developed in which electrically charged wires heated a pot. By 1891, iron plates used electrical elements.

1891
Electric kettle

The first electric kettle was invented in the USA in 1891. It boiled slowly and had fixed, non-renewable heating elements in the base.

Victorian schooling

In the early 19th century, there were no state-run schools, and no law to say children had to go to school. Few working-class children had any formal education. By the end of Victoria's reign, the government had recognized that working people needed an education, and made all children attend school until they were 13.

School funds

Church-run or charity schools provided education for the poor, but parents often could not afford to let their children stop work to attend. In 1870, a national system of Board Schools was set up, funded out of local rates (taxes).

Pupils faced the blackboard and copied lessons on to a slate using slate pencils

Dinner time at a ragged school

Slates were used in schools as they were cheaper than paper

Ragged schools
Founded in 1780 by philanthropist Robert Raikes, Sunday Schools for the poor spread rapidly. Known as "ragged schools", they provided free basic instruction, meals, and clothing for thousands of poor children until Board Schools replaced them with weekday education.

A white cotton apron kept school clothes clean

Not all parents could afford to buy school boots – some children went barefoot

Pupils sat in rows at metal-framed wooden desks

School subjects

To equip them for work, poor children were taught reading, writing, and arithmetic – the "three Rs". They also did sport, geography, and history. Girls learned how to cook; boys took woodwork lessons.

Religion and reading
In many schools, the school day, which ran from nine to five o'clock, began and ended with prayers. Pupils also read from the Bible and studied its teachings.

Children learned about the animal kingdom from this Bible

Public schools
Sons of rich families went to expensive public schools, such as Eton, Rugby, or Westminster (above). Pupils were taught classical subjects such as Latin and Greek, and educated to become leaders and statesmen. There were few schools for rich girls, who were taught mainly by governesses at home.

The properties of geometric shapes were learned by heart

Sphere

Pupils used a counting frame, or abacus, as a calculator

Cone

The ring was used to draw circles

Ring

Learning by heart
All children learned arithmetic, or mathematics. Teachers wrote maths problems on the blackboard, and the children copied them down. They learned by heart, chanting aloud their times tables and other facts, over and over again.

Teaching practice

Early Victorian teachers had little formal training and were poorly paid. Sometimes older pupils would repeat the lesson to the younger ones. From 1839, the government appointed school inspectors to check standards, and test children's progress.

Teachers used canes, or leather straps, to strike naughty pupils

Teacher's bamboo cane

Punishment
Discipline was strict. Pupils who did not learn their lessons stood in a corner, wearing a large cone-shaped hat called a dunce's cap. Talking was forbidden and teachers could hit children if they misbehaved.

Good attendance medal

Good attendance
Children often skipped school because they had to work, or look after younger children at home. In 1880, school became compulsory for all children aged 5 to 10 years old.

Education reforms
As industry grew, the state saw the need to educate working people, and introduced school reforms. These were mainly for children aged 5 to 13; after that, most working-class children went out to work.

1833
Government provides first grant to church schools.

1839
Government appoints first school inspectors.

1840
First teachers' training college opens in London.

1844
Factory Act states children in factories must have six half-days' schooling a week.

1870
Education Act sets up a nationwide system of Board Schools; their school fees are abolished in 1891.

1880
School is made compulsory for children aged 5 to 10; the leaving age is later raised to 13 years old.

1891
School fees abolished in Board Schools.

Art and architecture

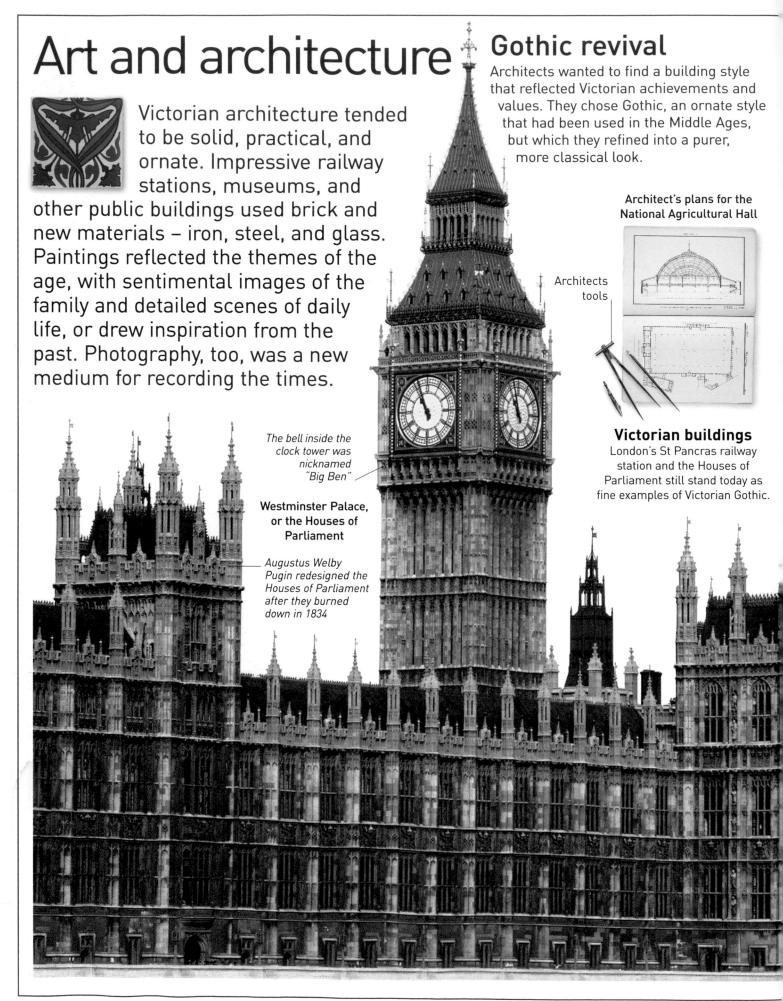

Victorian architecture tended to be solid, practical, and ornate. Impressive railway stations, museums, and other public buildings used brick and new materials – iron, steel, and glass. Paintings reflected the themes of the age, with sentimental images of the family and detailed scenes of daily life, or drew inspiration from the past. Photography, too, was a new medium for recording the times.

Gothic revival

Architects wanted to find a building style that reflected Victorian achievements and values. They chose Gothic, an ornate style that had been used in the Middle Ages, but which they refined into a purer, more classical look.

Architect's plans for the National Agricultural Hall

Architects tools

Victorian buildings

London's St Pancras railway station and the Houses of Parliament still stand today as fine examples of Victorian Gothic.

The bell inside the clock tower was nicknamed "Big Ben"

Westminster Palace, or the Houses of Parliament

Augustus Welby Pugin redesigned the Houses of Parliament after they burned down in 1834

Visual arts

The middle classes loved the romance of the past, as well as colourful scenes of everyday life. The age produced fine artists including John Everett Millais, William Holman Hunt, and Edward Burne-Jones.

J. W. Waterhouse's
The Lady of Shalott

Art for all

Until the 19th century, art had been an aristocratic interest. Now the Victorians built public art galleries like the one featured above in *The Picture Gallery* by James Hayllar.

Pre-Raphaelite Brotherhood

Founded in 1848, the Pre-Raphaelite Brotherhood illustrated poetry, moral, religious, and medieval themes in romantic paintings full of nature and light.

This scene is based on an Arthurian legend

Photography

In the 1830s, William Fox Talbot invented a successful photographic process. Later, the simple "Brownie" camera led to a boom in amateur photography.

Chemicals

Negative

Wet-plate camera

Telling a story

The Victorians liked paintings that told a moral story – to show how unfaithfulness, drunkenness, or (as seen here) the debts of a spendthrift could destroy family life.

Sepia prints

The Last Day in the Old Home by Robert Braithwaite Martineau

Families posed against formal studio backgrounds

William Morris

Arts and Crafts movement

William Morris was a member of the Pre-Raphaelite Brotherhood and criticized the social injustice, mass production, and ugliness of industrialism. His design firm used traditional handcrafts to produce wallpaper, furniture, silver, and fabrics of great simplicity. Morris believed people should be surrounded by things that combined beauty and usefulness. Known as Arts and Crafts, the style was very influential and is still popular today.

Morris-style ceramic tile

Ironically, Morris's designs were copied and mass produced

William Morris wallpaper

Books for all

The Victorians loved reading. Without cinema or television, books were a real source of pleasure and information. Greater educational opportunities increased the demand for books. Steam printing lowered the cost of production. Railway bookstalls, owned by W. H. Smith, and a growing number of libraries meant that books were more widely available.

A literate nation

Self-improvement was part of working-class culture and most people learned to read and write. Adults without a formal education attended local mechanics' institutes and other associations.

Public libraries
Access to libraries was originally limited to the wealthy. Workers clubbed together to buy books; sometimes rich philanthropists provided libraries. In 1850, the Public Libraries Act enabled towns to use rates to build free public libraries for all.

Dickens

Charles Dickens' first novel, *The Pickwick Papers*, was a hit and was followed by many others. He had known real poverty as a child, and wrote with compassion and humour about social injustices.

Illustrated instalment of Dickens' *Oliver Twist*

Monthly episodes
Dickens' novels were serialized in magazines, in monthly episodes, before being published in book form. Full of suspense, each episode left his public waiting eagerly for the next instalment.

Dickens is using a quill pen – a feather made into a pen

Charles Dickens at his writing desk

New genres

The Victorian age produced some of the finest novels in the English language. There was something for every taste, from Mrs Gaskell's *Mary Barton*, a moving story of life in the industrial north, to the Gothic horrors of Bram Stoker's *Dracula*.

Charlotte Brontë

Sherlock Holmes is one of fiction's greatest sleuths

Illustration from *Tess of the d'Urbervilles*

"TESS OF THE D'URBERVILLES"
By THOMAS HARDY

Brontë sisters

Charlotte, Anne, and Emily Brontë were born in Yorkshire. They wrote romantic novels. Charlotte is best known for *Jane Eyre*; Emily for *Wuthering Heights*; and Anne for *The Tenant of Wildfell Hall*.

Thomas Hardy

Hardy set his work against the backdrop of a disappearing countryside. Victorians were shocked by his later novels, such as *Tess of the d'Urbervilles*, because they described human relationships too realistically.

Daily papers

A popular press

The Times dated back to 1785, but it was expensive and catered for the upper classes. Newspapers were taxed, and there were harsh laws about content. In 1855, after a long battle for press freedom, the tax was removed, and newspapers became cheaper. They rolled non-stop off the new printing presses, and soon everyone was reading a paper. Comics appeared, too.

Detective fiction

As police became part of daily life, detective novels appeared. Wilkie Collins' *The Moonstone* featured the first detective hero in English fiction. Arthur Conan Doyle thrilled audiences with *The Adventures of Sherlock Holmes*.

Alice

Alice grows taller after drinking from a bottle

For children

A growing number of books were just for children. Some provided examples of how boys and girls should behave, but abiding favourites included Edward Lear's nonsense verse, Robert Louis Stephenson's *Treasure Island*, Rudyard Kipling's two *Jungle Books*, and *Black Beauty* by Anna Sewell.

Lewis Carroll

The first real fantasy tale for children was *Alice's Adventures in Wonderland*. It was written by Lewis Carroll, whose real name was Charles Dodgson, for a friend's daughters.

Dickens' novel David Copperfield was based on his own early life and poverty

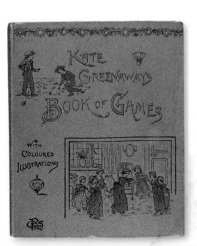

KATE GREENAWAY'S BOOK OF GAMES
WITH COLOURED ILLUSTRATIONS

Drawing by Kate Greenaway

Words and pictures

During the 1860s, children's picture books appeared in every middle-class nursery. Kate Greenaway illustrated everything from alphabets to verses. Most of them featured children.

Social reform

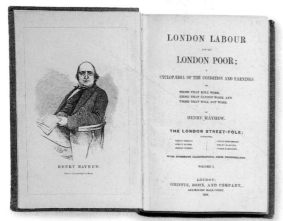

Industrialization created a wealthy middle class based on trade and industry. It also created a huge working class, much of which lived in terrible conditions. Poverty and human suffering were widespread. Official reports regularly investigated social problems, public concern grew, and major reforms were introduced.

Private philanthropy

Private or church-funded charity came before state help. Individual philanthropists spent their lives helping the needy by raising money and setting up soup kitchens, hostels, and orphanages.

Salvation Army bonnet

A religious army

In 1865, Methodist minister William Booth founded what later became the Salvation Army. Run on military lines, it provided shelter, clothes, and food for the destitute.

Social workers

Many middle-class women became involved in good works and were forerunners of today's social workers.

Mrs Fry reading to prisoners

Blowing the whistle

In the 1840s, observer Friedrich Engels described dire living conditions in Manchester. In the 1890s, reformers Charles Booth and Seebohm Rowntree estimated that at least 20 per cent of the population did not have enough to live on.

LONDON LABOUR
AND THE
LONDON POOR;
A CYCLOPÆDIA OF THE CONDITION AND EARNINGS
OF
THOSE THAT WILL WORK,
THOSE THAT CANNOT WORK, AND
THOSE THAT WILL NOT WORK.
BY
HENRY MAYHEW.

THE LONDON STREET-FOLK;

VOLUME I.

LONDON:
GRIFFIN, BOHN, AND COMPANY,
STATIONERS' HALL COURT.

HENRY MAYHEW.

Survey on the very poor

In *London Labour and the London Poor*, Henry Mayhew described how poverty drove people to prostitution and living off refuse.

Medicine and health

In 1842, a report showed that more than half the towns in Britain had impure water supplies. Cholera epidemics killed thousands. Gradually, the link between dirt and disease was understood, leading to reforms in medicine and public health.

1846
Ether inhaler
In 1846, long before painkillers were used, an American dentist used ether to make patients unconscious; soon surgeons took up the new anaesthetic.

1855
Stethoscope
In 1819, French doctor René Laennec had invented a tube for listening to a patient's heartbeat. By 1855, it had developed into a stethoscope.

Model housing

Many rich people tried to deal with the problems of slum housing and homelessness. US banker George Peabody gave £100,000 to provide "new model dwellings" with gardens for London's poor. Dr Barnardo founded homes for destitute children.

Peabody Square, Westminster

Peabody's houses were light and airy

Women prisoners took their children into prison so that they would not end up on the streets

Elizabeth Fry

Shocked by filthy conditions in London's Newgate Prison, Elizabeth Fry, a Quaker, formed an association that helped women prisoners find work and educated their children.

Public reform

The middle class believed in self-help, but governments had to take action. In 1875, a major public health act was passed; other laws improved working conditions and housing.

Lord Shaftesbury campaigned for Factory Acts, "ragged schools" and the plight of young chimney sweeps

Child labour

Some young boys worked as chimney sweeps, climbing up chimneys to remove soot. Many died from suffocation or severe burns. Charles Kingsley's novel, *The Water Babies*, publicized their suffering.

Chimney sweep's brush

Mealtime in a workhouse

Workhouses

Those who could not support themselves – mostly the unemployed or elderly – had to enter workhouses, where families were separated, food was bad, and work was meaningless. State pensions and benefits came in 1908.

1864
Dentist's drill

When fully wound, the new clockwork drill operated for up to two minutes at a time. It was noisy but fast. An electric drill soon followed, in 1875.

1867
Antiseptic spray

After Louis Pasteur had proved bacteria caused disease, surgeon Joseph Lister used a carbolic spray as an antiseptic to kill bacteria in wounds and on instruments.

1880

Endoscope

Victorian doctors developed this instrument for looking inside the body without cutting it open.

Fight for rights

Working people had no rights at the beginning of the Victorian period, and no vote. But as the century wore on, they began to fight back against hardship and exploitation. Through protest movements, trade unions, and other organizations, the working class demanded their right to better conditions, and a political voice.

Chartism

In 1838, a huge mass movement emerged and presented a People's Charter to Parliament, demanding the right to vote and other reforms. The demands were rejected, but most later became law.

Trade unions

When Chartism failed, workers turned to trade unions. In the 1850s, highly skilled workers – miners, railway workers, and engineers – formed powerful unions that could negotiate with employers who needed their labour. In the late 1880s, militant workers improved their conditions through strikes.

Membership certificate of the woodworkers' union

Parliament

Political power lay with Parliament. It consisted of an unelected, hereditary House of Lords and an elected House of Commons. Until the 1830s, members of Parliament represented only landowners, not the middle or working classes.

Political parties

The Conservative Party emerged in the 1830s from the old Tories. The Liberal Party emerged in the late 1850s from a mix of Whigs and radicals. Both parties competed for government. After 1867, they introduced social reforms to win the working-class vote. In 1893, socialist Keir Hardie founded the Independent Labour Party.

A meeting of the Women's Co-operative Guild, held at Burton-on-Trent

Interior of the House of Commons by Joseph Nash

Campaigning women

Women campaigned in the Chartist movement – demanding votes for both men and women – and formed their own trade unions. In 1883, married working-class women formed the Women's Co-operative Guild and went on to win maternity and other rights.

Voting card

New electorate

In 1832, middle-class men won the vote. Reform of Parliament began almost immediately, but it wasn't until 1867 and 1884 that the vote was given to many working-class men.

The new House of Commons was opened in 1852

After 1832, industrial towns such as Manchester and Sheffield could send MPs to Parliament

Almost half of all MPs still came from the landed gentry and aristocracy

Irish nationalism

Ireland was a major issue in Victorian politics. Poverty, land shortage, and dreadful famine in 1845–48 brought terrible hardship to the largely Catholic population. Irish nationalist groups, such as the Fenians, demanded Home Rule, or self-government, but Parliament rejected Home Rule bills in 1886 and in 1893.

There were no women MPs until 1918, when women were finally given the vote

---

Reform acts

In 1832, 435,000 men had the vote. By 1885, it had risen to 5.6 million men.

1832
Great Reform Act gives the vote to middle-class men; also creates new electoral districts in industrial towns.

1858
Property qualification for MPs is abolished; now non-landowners can be elected.

1867
The vote extends to most urban working-class men.

1872
Ballot Act: voters can cast votes in secret.

1884
The vote extends to most rural working-class men.

Leisure time

Life improved for most people during the second half of Queen Victoria's reign. Working hours shortened, wages rose, and prices of goods and food fell. From 1850, factories closed on Saturday afternoons and, in 1871, a new law introduced four official bank holidays a year. With money to spend, and time to spare, the Victorians created what was effectively the start of a leisure industry.

Seaside trips

Railways and cheap fares made seaside holidays possible. More and more people made day trips to the sea or, if they could afford it, stayed for a week or more. Blackpool was the first seaside town dedicated to the holiday trade.

Punch and Judy puppets

Beach life

Beaches were a hive of activity, with bathing huts, donkey rides, and Punch and Judy puppet shows. The Victorians built long metal piers where Pierrot (clown) shows and brass bands provided entertainment.

Thomas Cook poster advertising holidays abroad

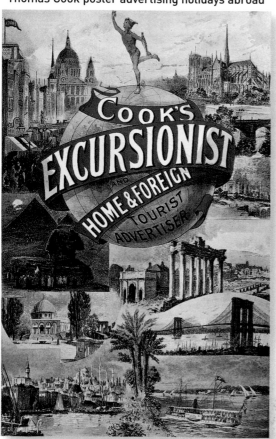

COOK'S EXCURSIONIST AND HOME & FOREIGN TOURIST ADVERTISER

Cook's tours

In 1841, Thomas Cook started a travel firm. By the 1880s, with the rise of steamships and continental railways, Cook's firm guided middle-class tourists around Europe, the Holy Land (Palestine), and Egypt's pyramids.

Gas lights illuminated the promenade

As resorts grew, guest houses and smart hotels sprang up

Ladies carried parasols for shade from the Sun

Men and women strolled along the promenade dressed in their Sunday best

Even on the hottest days, men, women, and children remained covered up

Promenades let visitors breathe in the sea air without having to walk on the sand

On the Promenade, Brighton by Theodore Hines

Music concerts

Middle-class audiences flocked to theatres and concert halls such as the Royal Albert Hall to hear music by Mendelssohn and Verdi, or light opera by Gilbert and Sullivan.

Musical programme

Music halls

Working-class music lovers went to music halls, or played in brass bands. By 1880, there were more than 500 music halls in Britain.

Public houses

Pubs were lively places, where working people could relax with friends and play games such as dominoes and cards.

London theatre poster

Sport for all

Sport was a national pastime. Cricket, rugby, and golf were all popular, and sportsmen, such as cricketer W. G. Grace, became national heroes. Lawn tennis began in 1874.

Leather football and rugby ball

Football

In 1863, the Football Association laid down national rules. Different areas formed clubs, and fans travelled by bus, tram, and train to support their team.

Wooden tennis racket

Dominoes

Playing cards

Lemonade bottle

Beer bottles

Cycling fun

In 1884, the "safety" bicycle appeared and cycling took off. By 1901, Britain had more than 2,000 cycling clubs.

Air-filled rubber tyres gave a smooth ride

Safety bicycle

All piers had a bandstand

Swimmers went into the sea from bathing huts

Empire-builders

When Victoria became Queen, Britain already governed parts of India, Canada, and Australia, and various overseas colonies. Together they formed the British Empire. From the 1870s, Britain set out to win new territories, markets, and influence, particularly in Africa. By 1901, Queen Victoria ruled nearly one-quarter of the world's people. The British Empire was the largest the world had ever seen.

Trading empire
The British Empire (shown in red) spread over every continent and was built on trade. Britain imported raw materials, such as cotton, tea, and rubber from the colonies and exported manufactured goods, from locomotives to machine tools, back to the colonies.

Jewel in the crown

India's resources, exotic peoples and regions, and long-standing links with Britain made it special – "the jewel in the crown" as Queen Victoria said. British involvement grew from trading stations set up by the East India Company in 1600. By 1900, an Anglo-Indian army and vast civil service governed virtually the entire subcontinent.

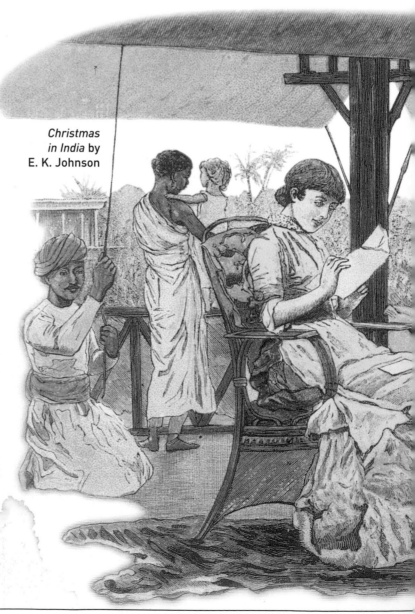

Christmas in India by E. K. Johnson

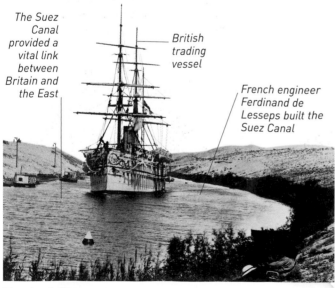

The Suez Canal provided a vital link between Britain and the East

British trading vessel

French engineer Ferdinand de Lesseps built the Suez Canal

East of Suez
From 1869, Egypt's Suez Canal linked the Mediterranean Sea and the Indian Ocean. Six years later, Britain bought the controlling interest in the canal. This shortened the route to India, increased Britain's access to the East, and, from 1882, gave Britain effective rule over Egypt.

Battle of Sepoys, India, 1857

Three regiments of sepoys mutinied

Indian mutiny

In 1857, Indian soldiers, or sepoys, rebelled against British army officers. After the terrible bloodshed, the British aimed to rule with greater sensitivity, but still saw India as a permanent part of the Empire. An independence movement emerged, and in 1885, the Indian National Congress met for the first time.

Scramble for Africa

In the 1870s, a "scramble for Africa" began. Britain, competing against France, Germany, and other empire-builders, gained the most: Kenya, Uganda, Nigeria, and southern Africa, including Rhodesia (Zimbabwe).

Missionaries

Victorian missionaries travelled through Africa and Asia preaching Christianity, but also setting up schools and hospitals. Scottish missionary David Livingstone spent 30 years in Africa, exploring the Zambezi region and working with local people.

David Livingstone

Livingstone's compass and magnifying glass

India offered career opportunities for British traders, soldiers, and administrators

Naturalists drew these insects in the Amazon region of South America

Exploration

British explorers travelled through countries hardly known by Europeans. They sent back specimens and accounts to new institutions such as the Royal Geographic Society.

Leaving home

Ford Madox Brown's *The Last of England* (above) shows a couple leaving Britain. From the 1850s, thousands of British and Irish emigrants set sail for the colonies – particularly Australia, Canada, and New Zealand – in search of a better life.

Going to war

British foreign policy aimed to defend, and expand, Britain's interests. Her troops were constantly in action, policing the Empire. They fought Māoris in New Zealand, Jamaicans in the Caribbean, and brutally crushed the Indian Mutiny. The horrors of the Crimean War shocked the public, but in Africa, defeats by the Sudanese at Khartoum in 1885, and the Zulus in 1879, caused a surge of patriotism. By 1899, Britain was engaged in a bitter conflict in South Africa, known as the Boer War.

Crimean War

The Crimean War of 1854–56 was fought by British, French, Turkish, and Sardinian forces to prevent Russian expansion into Turkish-controlled lands.

Both sides suffered dreadful casualties

The siege of Sebastapol
The allies defeated Russian forces at Alma, then laid siege to the Russian fortress of Sebastapol for nearly a year, through a bitterly cold winter. Newspaper reports fuelled public outrage at the length, horrors, and mismanagement of the war.

Boer War

In 1899, war broke out in South Africa between Dutch settlers, known as Boers, and Britain, for control of mineral-rich territories. Defeated at Mafeking, Kimberley, and Ladysmith, Britain sent huge reinforcements. They recaptured Mafeking, and the Boers were finally defeated in 1902.

British troops in action during the Boer War

British troops at Kimberley

Military technology
Victorian armies depended on horses to carry supplies, and soldiers. Bayonets remained common, but new breech-loading rifles, smokeless powder, and rapid-firing machine guns all transformed warfare. The rifles gave British soldiers a huge advantage over indigenous peoples.

New firearms were loaded from behind the barrel rather than in front

Photography and telegraphy brought home the realities of war for the first time

A mismanaged war

The British army in Crimea suffered from lack of preparation, conflicting orders, and shortage of supplies. At Balaclava, confused orders sent the British cavalry on a suicidal charge against massed Russian artillery. Nearly half the cavalry were killed or wounded. Tennyson's poem, *The Charge of the Light Brigade*, immortalized the disaster.

Royal Navy

The Victorians were proud of their navy, which was the largest and most powerful in the world. Industrial developments transformed naval warfare; by the 1880s, steam-driven ironclads (wooden warships with armour plating) and steamships were replacing wood and sail.

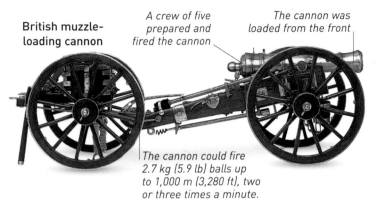

British muzzle-loading cannon

A crew of five prepared and fired the cannon

The cannon was loaded from the front

The cannon could fire 2.7 kg (5.9 lb) balls up to 1,000 m (3,280 ft), two or three times a minute.

Tommies

Khakis were a dull yellowish-brown colour

By the 1890s, the ordinary British soldier had acquired a new status, and a nickname: Tommy Atkins. British soldiers also had a new uniform – khaki – which provided better camouflage than the red coats worn previously.

Victoria Cross

Queen Victoria instituted the medal in 1856

Medal is made out of bronze from Russian cannons

Soldiers of the Queen

The Crimean war focused public opinion on the ordinary soldier. Britain's standing army was quite small, and troops were treated badly. From the 1860s, reforms were introduced and brutal practices, such as flogging, were outlawed. Medals were awarded to all ranks, and the Victoria Cross was created for outstanding bravery.

Field hospitals

More soldiers died of disease and infection in Crimea than of their wounds. Hygiene and medical supplies were almost unknown. In 1855, Florence Nightingale arrived in Scutari with a handful of women nurses. She demanded supplies, introduced sanitation, and created the first effective military hospital. In doing so, she revolutionized nursing.

End of an era

In 1901, Queen Victoria died. Her reign had seen extraordinary change. Great industrial towns and cities had emerged. Trains ran through the countryside and steamships lined the docks. Shops sold previously unimaginable goods, made in British factories or imported from Britain's worldwide empire. Most people were now better fed, healthier, and more educated.

An uncertain future

The Victorians' energy and innovation made them world leaders. But in 1901, Britain was no longer the world's leading power. Since the 1870s, the United States and Germany had industrialized, and were rapidly overtaking Britain. Poverty was still widespread, Britain was at war, and there were problems in the British Empire.

Death of a Queen
In 1897, Britain celebrated Queen Victoria's Diamond Jubilee – 60 years on the throne. Just over three years later, Victoria died aged 81. Her coffin was carried on a gun carriage through London. Thousands of mourners from Britain and the Empire lined the streets to watch it pass.

The legacy

The Victorians transformed Britain from an agricultural country to a world industrial power, excelling in industry, engineering, science, public health, and education. Victorian technology, empire-building, and values also influenced the rest of the world, sometimes with damaging effects.

Lasting monuments

Victorians built things to last, and Britain today is full of their public buildings, statues, train stations, bridges, and even seaside piers. From family life to foreign travel, their impact on daily life was huge. Much of what we have today – from telephones and light bulbs to sports and modern medicine – came from the Victorians.

The Queen Victoria Memorial stands in front of Buckingham Palace, London

Postal service

Victorians not only developed trains, buses, and trams, but also our postal service. From 1840, anyone sending a letter had to pay in advance. The first postage stamp cost one old penny, and was known as a "Penny Black".

Penny Black

Challenges

In 1859, Charles Darwin published *On the Origin of Species*, suggesting that all life forms had evolved over millions of years, and that humans might be descended from apes. His views shocked many God-fearing Victorians who took the Bible literally and believed in an unchanging world.

Charles Darwin

The Victoria and Albert Museum, London, started in 1899

The museum houses art and culture from around the world

Education for all

Learning of all kinds had once been restricted to a privileged minority. The Victorians recognized that an industrial population needed access to free education, and to culture. They built not only schools but also museums, libraries, and art galleries that still stand today.

In the 1890s, three out of every four ships in the world were built in British shipyards

Co-operation, not competition

Early socialists saw industrialism as a contest between profit and labour, and sought to build a new society. First set up in the 1840s, co-op shops aimed to provide food and other goods at prices that working people could afford.

Co-op department store, c. 1900

World impact

During Victorian times, the world became more accessible. Trade, improved transport, and better communications meant that exotic places, foods, and even foreign words became part of daily life.

Pride and patriotism

Many Victorians believed the Empire would last for ever, and the progress they had made – in industry and engineering, medicine and education – would benefit everyone. Even popular songs and team sports emphasized determination, fair play, and the superiority of British values.

Bolton Wanderers Football Club

Team sports are a popular legacy from the Victorian period

As today, the Victorians believed that sport encouraged health, competitiveness, and team spirit

Important dates

1837	Victoria ascends to the throne
1840s	Railway "mania" hits Britain
1842	Mines Act bans women and children from underground work in mines
1844	Factory Act prevents children under nine from working in factories
1845–48	Potato famine in Ireland: nearly a million die and thousands emigrate
1848	Public Health Act sets up board of health to improve sanitation in towns
1851	Great Exhibition held in London; celebrates Victorian achievements
1851	Amalgamated Society of Engineers, the engineering union, founded
1854–56	Crimean War in Russia; 4,600 soldiers die in battle; 13,000 are wounded; 17,500 die of disease
1869	John Sainsbury opens a small grocery shop in London; it later develops into a nationwide chain of shops
1870	Forster's Education Act makes primary education available for all
1870s	Cheap, imported foodstuffs transform daily diet
1875	Artisans Dwelling Act enables local authorities to pull down and replace slum dwellings
1881	First electric street lighting appears
1882	Married Women's Property Act enables married women to have legal ownership over their property
1890	Electric trains run on London's underground railway
1891	Primary education in state schools becomes free
1895	Herbert Austin opens motor car factory in Birmingham
1899–1902	Boer War in South Africa
1901	Queen Victoria dies aged 81

Facts and figures

The Victorian Age lasted from 1837 to 1901, when Queen Victoria reigned. To help you find out more about this fascinating period, these pages provide useful facts and figures, key dates, and a list of places to visit (see also pp. 46–47).

Population boom
As Victorian Britain changed from an agricultural to an industrial society, towns and cities grew rapidly, and the population soared. From the middle of the century, improvements in housing, sanitation, diet, and health accelerated this growth.

Population in Great Britain in millions

1837	1851	1901
18	21	37

The royal family tree
Queen Victoria's father was the younger brother of George IV and William IV. She came to the throne in 1837, and married her cousin Albert in 1840. They had nine children. Their eldest son, "Bertie", succeeded Victoria as Edward VII in 1901. His great granddaughter is Elizabeth II, who was crowned in 1953.

House of Hanover

EDWARD, DUKE OF KENT
(1767–1820)
MARRIED VICTORIA OF SAXE-SAALFIELD-COBURG

VICTORIA
(1819–1901)
QUEEN OF GREAT BRITAIN AND IRELAND 1837–1901, EMPRESS OF INDIA 1877–1901
MARRIED ALBERT OF SAXE-COBURG-GOTHA

VICTORIA, PRINCESS ROYAL
(1840–1901)
MARRIED KAISER FRIEDRICH OF GERMANY

ALICE, GRAND DUCHESS OF HESSE-DARMSTADT
(1843–78)
MARRIED LOUIS GRAND DUKE OF HESSE

HELENA, PRINCESS OF SCHLESWIG-HOLSTEIN
(1846–1923)
MARRIED PRINCE CHRISTIAN OF SCHLESWIG-HOLSTEIN

EDWARD VII
(1841–1910)
KING OF GREAT BRITAIN AND IRELAND, KING OF THE DOMINIONS BEYOND THE SEAS, EMPEROR OF INDIA 1901–10
MARRIED PRINCESS ALEXANDRA OF DENMARK

ALFRED, DUKE OF EDINBURGH
(1844–1900)
MARRIED GRAND DUCHESS MARIE ALEXANDROVNA OF RUSSIA

PRIME MINISTERS FROM 1835 TO 1901

1835–41

VISCOUNT MELBOURNE
Whig

1841–46

ROBERT PEEL
Conservative

18

LORD JOHN RUSSELL
Liberal

1852
EARL OF DERBY
Conservative

1852–55
EARL OF ABERDEEN
Peelite
(Supporter of Robert Peel)

1855–58

VISCOUNT PALMERSTON
Liberal

1858–59
EARL OF DERBY
Conservative

1859–65
VISCOUNT PALMERSTON
Liberal

Railway boom

The map shows the growth of British railways between 1825 and 1851, which is when most of our present-day system was built. Following the railway "mania" of the 1840s, the network expanded from 3,123 km (1,940 miles) of track in 1843 to more than 20,920 km (13,000 miles) by 1870.

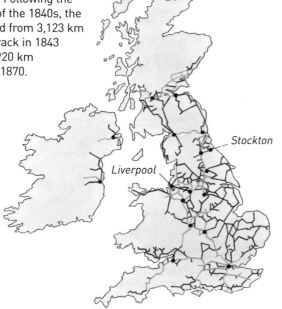

Railway key:

Stockton to Darlington 1825

Liverpool to Manchester 1830

Railway lines by 1844

Railway lines by 1851

Stockton

Liverpool

House of Coburg

ERNEST I, DUKE OF COBURG
(1784–1844)
MARRIED LOUISE OF SAXE-GOTHA

**ERNEST II,
DUKE OF COBURG**
(1818–93)

ALBERT, DUKE OF SAXE-COBURG-GOTHA
(1819–61)
PRINCE CONSORT OF GREAT BRITAIN AND IRELAND 1840–61
MARRIED QUEEN VICTORIA OF GREAT BRITAIN AND IRELAND

**ARTHUR,
DUKE OF CONNAUGHT**
(1850–1942)
*MARRIED PRINCESS LOUISE
OF PRUSSIA*

**BEATRICE,
PRINCESS OF BATTENBERG**
(1857–1944)
*MARRIED PRINCE HENRY
OF BATTENBERG*

**LOUISE,
DUCHESS OF ARGYLL**
(1848–1939)
*MARRIED JOHN CAMPBELL,
DUKE OF ARGYLL*

**LEOPOLD,
DUKE OF ALBANY**
(1853–84)
*MARRIED PRINCESS
HELENA OF WALDECK*

Museums to visit

Reconstruction of a Victorian chemist's at Blists Hill

Bethnal Green Museum of Childhood, London (toys, puppets, and doll's houses)

Big Pit Mining Museum, Torfaen, Wales (underground tours, workshops, and exhibitions)

Blists Hill Victorian Town, Ironbridge Gorge Museum, Ironbridge, Shropshire (50-acre working Victorian town)

Greater Manchester Police, Manchester (Victorian police station, cells, and museum)

Museum of Childhood, Edinburgh (toys, puzzles, books, and chimney sweeps)

National Railway Museum, York (famous trains and 300 years of railway history)

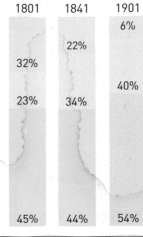

Noah's Ark from Museum of Childhood, Edinburgh

People's History Museum, Manchester (reconstructs 200 years of social and labour history)

Yesterday's World, Battle, East Sussex (over 100,000 exhibits of domestic life (1850–1950)

York Castle Museum, York (reconstructed Victorian street with stocked shops)

Inside Greater Manchester Police Station

Working patterns

In 1801, nearly a third of the working population were employed in farming. By 1901, that figure had dropped to six per cent, and 40 per cent worked in industry. A large number worked in the service industries, such as domestic service, medicine, and banking.

	1801	1841	1901
Services	23%	34%	40%
Industry	32%	22%	6%
Agriculture	45%	44%	54%

Employment key:

 Services   Industry   Agriculture

1865–66
LORD JOHN RUSSELL
Liberal

1866–68
EARL OF DERBY
Conservative

1868

BENJAMIN DISRAELI
Conservative

WILLIAM EWART GLADSTONE
Liberal

1868–74

1874
BENJAMIN DISR.
Conservative

1880–85
**WILLIAM EWART
GLADSTONE**
Liberal

1885–86
**MARQUIS OF
SALISBURY**
Conservative

1886
**WILLIAM EWART
GLADSTONE**
Liberal

1886–92
**MARQUIS OF
SALISBURY**
Conservative

1892–94
**WILLIAM EWART
GLADSTONE**
Liberal

1894–95
5TH EARL ROSEBERY
Liberal

1895–1902
**MARQUIS OF
SALISBURY**
Conservative

Did you know?

AMAZING FACTS

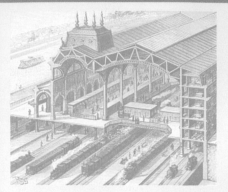

A busy Victorian railway station

Before the Victorian period, each town set its own time. It was the coming of the railways and the need to have a national train timetable that forced the country to adopt one standard time. The correct time was usually displayed on a public clock at the station or on the town hall, and everyone set their watches from this.

The Victorians were very modest about their bodies. Ladies in particular were careful to keep their legs covered up at all times – allowing a gentleman to see even their ankles was considered most improper. Even to go swimming, they wore costumes with ankle-length trousers.

The first trip organized by Thomas Cook, founder of the famous travel company, was a one-day outing from Leicester to Loughborough for a picnic in 1841. By the 1880s, he was taking people to much more exotic destinations around Europe, and even as far as Egypt.

Our phrase "in the limelight" comes from the Victorian theatre. Lights that burned lime were used as footlights at the front of the stage. They produced a very bright light, which was often used to spotlight the leading characters. If actors got too close to these lights, they could burn the bottom of their costumes.

Most Victorian factory workers lived close to their factory, and often the noise of the boilers or machinery starting up in the morning would be enough to wake them up. Some mines and factories employed people called "knockers-up", whose job was to bang on the workers' doors each morning to get them up in time for work.

Buffalo Bill's Wild West Show was a popular four-hour spectacle starring the popular American heroes "Buffalo Bill", Big Chief Sitting Bull, and sharpshooter Annie Oakley. The show featured native American war dances, shooting displays, and an enactment of an attack on a stagecoach.

The Victorians invented buckets and spades for playing on the beach, deck chairs, piers, and going for a walk along the prom. Even the ice cream cornet was first sold to Victorians.

Many places around the world are named after Queen Victoria. The state of Victoria in Australia, Lake Victoria and the Victoria Falls in Africa, the city of Victoria in British Columbia, Canada, and the Victoria Mountains in New Zealand are just some of her namesakes.

At the start of Queen Victoria's reign, half of all the babies born in Britain died before they reached the age of five. The main child-killing diseases were cholera, typhoid, and diarrhoea.

Victorian town hall clock

A poster advertising Buffalo Bill's Wild West Show

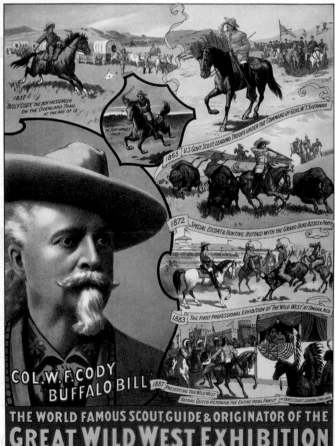

1857 BILLY CODY THE BOY MESSENGER ON THE OVERLAND TRAIL AT THE AGE OF 12

THE PONY EXPRESS RIDER

1865 U.S. GOVT. SCOUT, LEADING TROOPS UNDER THE COMMAND OF GEN. W. T. SHERMAN

1872 SPECIAL ESCORT & HUNTING BUFFALO WITH THE GRAND DUKE ALEXIS & PARTY

1883 THE FIRST PROFESSIONAL EXHIBITION OF THE WILD WEST AT OMAHA, NEB

COL. W. F. CODY BUFFALO BILL

1887 PRESENTING THE WILD WEST BEFORE QUEEN VICTORIA & THE ENTIRE ROYAL FAMILY AT EARL'S COURT, LONDON, ENGLAND

THE WORLD FAMOUS SCOUT, GUIDE & ORIGINATOR OF THE GREAT WILD WEST EXHIBITION

QUESTIONS AND ANSWERS

Stained-glass window of Queen Victoria

Q Was Queen Victoria always popular among her subjects?

A Queen Victoria survived at least seven attempts to assassinate her, but her Golden and Diamond Jubilees were celebrated around the Empire, and thousands of people crowded into London to watch her funeral in 1901.

Q How did Victorians show that they were in mourning?

A When someone died, their family would go into a period of mourning. They wore dark, sombre clothes and special mourning jewellery, often made of a black gemstone called jet.

Q How did Victorian ladies get such big skirts?

A In the 1850s, ladies began to widen their skirts by wearing a metal cage called a crinoline. This was covered with several petticoats, and then a dress.

A Victorian lady wearing a crinoline

Q Why was the cotton weaving industry so successful in Britain?

A From the 1770s, new steam-powered machines made it quick and cheap to spin and weave cotton. The centre of the industry was in Lancashire. At one point, there were 100,000 cotton looms in the Lancashire town of Burnley alone.

Q How did British soldiers get the nickname "Tommies"?

A Each new recruit was given a form in which to record his name, age, and so on. The example that showed men how to fill in the form gave the name Thomas Atkins – hence "Tommies".

Q Why did so many Victorians die from diseases such as cholera and typhoid?

A At first, people thought these diseases were inhaled, and blamed bad-smelling air. Then, in 1854, the London doctor John Snow proved that a cholera outbreak had been caused by people drinking infected water from a public water pump. Public health improved dramatically when a network of new water pipes and sewers was built soon after to keep the water clean.

Record breakers

BIGGEST SHIPS
In 1837, Isambard Kingdom Brunel's steam-powered *Great Western* was the world's biggest ship, measuring 64.6 m (212 ft) from bow to stern. His *Great Eastern* of 1858 was even bigger, at 211 m (692 ft) in length.

RECORD-BREAKING MONARCH
Victoria was the first British queen to be photographed, filmed, and shown on stamps. She ruled about one-fifth of the world, and almost a quarter of its people.

SUCCESS STORY
The Great Exhibition drew six million visitors in 1851 and made enough profit to pay for several new museums and colleges, including the Natural History Museum, Imperial College, and the Victoria and Albert Museum.

The Natural History Museum, London

Some famous Victorians

The Victorians made huge strides in science, the arts, industry, politics, social reform, and many other areas. Here are just some of the people responsible.

Statue of Thomas Hardy

WRITERS AND ARTISTS

• The Brontës
Yorkshire's Brontë sisters, Charlotte (1816–55), Emily (1818–48), and Anne (1820–49), wrote romantic novels. The best-known are *Jane Eyre*, written by Charlotte, *Wuthering Heights* by Emily, and *The Tenant of Wildfell Hall* by Anne.

• Edward Burne-Jones (1833–98)
Pre-Raphaelite painter and designer, often inspired by medieval tales. Also famous for his tapestries and stained-glass windows for churches.

• Lewis Carroll (1832–98)
Writer (real name Charles Dodgson) and mathematics lecturer at Oxford University. He wrote *Alice's Adventures in Wonderland* and nonsense verse such as *The Hunting of the Snark*.

From *A Christmas Carol*, by Dickens

• Wilkie Collins (1824–89)
Credited with inventing the detective novel. His most famous books are *The Woman in White* and *The Moonstone*, which featured the first ever detective hero in English fiction – Sergeant Cuff.

• Charles Dickens (1812–70)
The Victorians' favourite novelist. Most of his novels were serialized in newspapers or magazines – each episode ended with a cliffhanger, so readers were desperate for the next episode. His best-known novels include *The Pickwick Papers*, *A Christmas Carol*, *David Copperfield*, and *Great Expectations*.

• Arthur Conan Doyle (1859–1930)
The world-famous fictional detective Sherlock Holmes and his assistant, Dr Watson, first appeared in the story *A Study in Scarlet* in 1887, and became a huge success with the public.

• George Eliot (1819–80)
Novelist (real name Mary Ann Evans) whose best known books include *Adam Bede*, *The Mill on the Floss*, and *Middlemarch*. Her early works often focused on rural life, whereas *Middlemarch* was set in a provincial town.

• Thomas Hardy (1840–1928)
Dorset novelist who wrote about country life at a key moment, when mechanization was about to destroy ancient farming methods for ever. His most famous novels include *Far from the Madding Crowd*, *Tess of the D'Urbervilles*, and *Jude the Obscure*.

• William Holman Hunt (1827–1910)
Painter and member of the Pre-Raphaelite Brotherhood. Hunt's first big success, in 1854, was *The Light of the World*, which showed Jesus knocking at the door to a human soul. Later paintings included *The Triumph of the Innocents* and *May Morning on Magdalen Tower*.

• John Everett Millais (1829–96)
Pre-Raphaelite painter. Among his best-known works are *Christ in the House of His Parents*, *Ophelia*, *The Order of Release*, and *The Blind Girl*.

• William Morris (1834–96)
Designer, craftsman, poet, and early socialist. His furniture, fabrics, and wallpaper were produced using traditional techniques. This style became known as "Arts and Crafts".

• The Rosettis
Dante Gabriel Rosetti (1828–82) was a Pre-Raphaelite painter and poet. His sister, Christina (1830–94), was also a poet, writing ballads and love poetry in a technically advanced style.

Wallpaper designed by William Morris

PHILANTHROPISTS AND SOCIAL REFORMERS

A public water supply in 1863

• Edwin Chadwick (1800–90)
Doctor and public health reformer. Chadwick's *Report on the Sanitary Condition of the Labouring Population of Great Britain* in 1842 was the first detailed survey of public health. His campaign for reform led to the first Public Health Act of 1848.

• John Stuart Mill (1806–73)
Philosopher and social reformer. His *On Liberty* stated that a good government should encourage individual liberty – the basis for modern democracy. As an MP, he supported women's rights, including the right to vote.

• Florence Nightingale (1820–1910)
Nurse and founder of trained nursing as a profession. During the Crimean War, her policies of cleanliness and sanitation saved many soldiers' lives.

• Annie Besant (1847–1933)
Campaigner for birth control, women's rights, and women's trade union rights. In 1888, Besant was involved with a strike to improve the conditions of women workers in match factories.

• Josephine Butler (1828–1906)
Campaigner against prostitution and the exploitation of women. She fought to repeal the Contagious Diseases Acts, which forced female prostitutes – but not their male clients – in naval and military towns to be tested for sexually transmitted diseases.

• Elizabeth Garrett Anderson (1836–1917)
The first woman in Britain to qualify as a doctor, gain membership of the British Medical Association, and become a mayor and magistrate.

• Keir Hardie (1856–1915)
Socialist, labour leader, and the first MP to represent working men and women. In 1893, Hardie founded the forerunner of today's Labour Party.

• Octavia Hill (1838–1912)
Social reformer who was particularly involved in slum clearance and building better houses for the poor.

• Lord Shaftesbury (1801–85)
Factory reformer and MP. His campaigns led to women, girls, and boys under the age of ten being banned from working in coal mines, and to the working day in textile mills being limited to ten hours. He also set up free "ragged schools" for the destitute.

Bust of Florence Nightingale

ENGINEERS AND INVENTORS

• Alexander Graham Bell (1847–1922)
Scottish-American inventor. Interested in transmitting sounds by electricity, in 1876, Bell patented the first telephone. He also worked on such diverse areas as the phonograph, aerial vehicles, and teaching speech to the deaf.

Manufacturing Bessemer steel

• Henry Bessemer (1813–98)
Inventor and engineer who developed the Bessemer process – a fast, cheap way to manufacture steel in bulk.

• Jesse Boot (1850–1931)
English drug manufacturer, and founder of the Boots chain store. Boot opened his first shop in Nottingham in 1877, and by mass-selling at low prices effectively started the chain store.

• Isambard Kingdom Brunel (1806–59)
One of Britain's greatest engineers. Brunel created the Great Western Railway, the Clifton Suspension Bridge in Bristol, and three record-breaking ships: the *Great Western*, the *Great Britain*, and the *Great Eastern*.

• John Boyd Dunlop (1840–1921)
Inventor of the pneumatic tyre and founder of the Dunlop Rubber Company to manufacture pneumatic bicycle tyres.

• William Fox Talbot (1800–77)
Pioneer photographer who invented an early form of photograph, called the calotype, in 1840.

An 1835 "mousetrap" camera, as used by Fox Talbot

Find out more

In Britain, we are surrounded by reminders of the Victorian period. Look out for Victorian buildings close to where you live, or streets with names like "Victoria", "Albert", and "Wellington". Some famous museums are listed here and on p. 41, but your local museum may also have a Victorian collection that is worth visiting.

Around your town

Most British towns have a wealth of Victorian buildings – from town halls, schools, or churches to mills, factories, or other industrial buildings – as well as statues of famous politicians, great military leaders, and, of course, of Queen Victoria herself. See what Victorian treasures you can spot in your town.

Statue of Queen Victoria outside Windsor Castle

Visit a museum

Some museums, such as the Victoria and Albert Museum, have big collections of objects and clothes from the Victorian period. There are also museums where you can see Victorian industrial equipment in action, and Victorian houses that are open to the public. See the "Places to Visit" box, opposite.

The Victoria and Albert Museum, in London

A terrace of Victorian houses

Victorian houses

If you live in a British town, you may live near (or even on) a street lined with Victorian houses. Typical features to look out for include: a bay window at the front, sash windows (windows that push up and down), and the use of different coloured bricks for decoration.

Landmarks

Many of Britain's most famous buildings are Victorian. For example, the Lancashire town of Blackpool became a popular seaside resort during the Victorian period, and the tower, piers, and other landmarks were all built at this time.

Blackpool Tower

In your own home

Can openers, vacuum cleaners, electric irons, and kettles are just some of the useful items invented by the Victorians. They were also the first to install flushing toilets in their houses.

An early flushing toilet, from the Victorian period

USEFUL WEBSITES

Website on Victorian children's daily life:
www.bbc.co.uk/schools/primaryhistory/victorian_britain/

Excellent site on Victorian Britain:
www.bbc.co.uk/history/trail/victorian_britain/

Information on technology during the Victorian era:
www.bbc.co.uk/history/british/victorians/victorian_technology_01.shtml

PLACES TO VISIT

VICTORIA AND ALBERT MUSEUM, LONDON

Contains a huge collection of porcelain, tapestries, jewellery, glass, clothes, paintings, and photographs from all over the world. Star Victorian exhibits include the Morris, Gamble, and Poynter rooms, which were decorated by (and named after) three designers who recreated historic styles using the materials of the industrial age.

QUEEN STREET MILL, BURNLEY

At this steam-powered cotton mill, visitors can see the 500-horsepower steam engine and the weaving looms in action.

ARMLEY MILLS MUSEUM, LEEDS

A 19th-century woollen mill, with working looms, water wheels, and spinning "mules".

THE MUSEUM OF WELSH LIFE, ST FAGANS, OUTSIDE CARDIFF

At this open-air museum, look out for:
- a Victorian bakehouse where bread and cakes are still cooked daily
- a grocery shop
- a rural school
- a terrace of iron workers' cottages.

SS *GREAT BRITAIN*, BRISTOL

The SS *Great Britain*, designed by Brunel, was the world's first large iron passenger ship. It sits in Bristol's Great Western dock.

SALTAIRE, NEAR BRADFORD

This model industrial village, completed in 1873, was built by Sir Titus Salt to house the workers employed in his textile mill.

SOME FAMOUS VICTORIAN BUILDINGS:
- London's Houses of Parliament, St Pancras Station, Albert Memorial, and Natural History Museum
- Manchester's Rotunda and Museum of Science and Industry
- Blackpool Tower and piers
- Brighton Palace Pier
- The Clifton Suspension Bridge, Bristol
- Leed's town hall and shopping arcades
- The Forth Rail Bridge, outside Edinburgh
- The Scott Monument, Edinburgh
- Cardiff Castle

Victorian doll